Franz Joseph Haydn

Missa in Angustiis
Nelson Mass

VOCAL SCORE

Edited by

DENIS McCALDIN

Music Department
OXFORD UNIVERSITY PRESS
Oxford and New York

Oxford University Press, Great Clarendon Street, Oxford OX2 6DP
Oxford University Press Inc., 198 Madison Avenue, New York, NY 10016, USA

Oxford New York
Athens Auckland Bangkok Bombay
Calcutta Cape Town Dar es Salaam Delhi
Florence Hong Kong Istanbul Karachi
Kuala Lumpur Madras Madrid Melbourne
Mexico City Nairobi Paris Singapore
Taipei Tokyo Toronto
and associated companies in
Berlin Ibadan

Oxford is a trade mark of Oxford University Press

17

ISBN 978-0-19-336789-0

Printed in Great Britain on acid-free paper by Halstan & Co. Ltd., Amersham, Bucks.

Full scores, vocal scores, and instrumental parts
are available for hire from the publisher's hire library.

Scoring (original version 1798): 3 trumpets, timpani, strings, and organ.

Scoring (revised version, Haydn/Fuchs *c.*1800): flute, 2 oboes, 2 clarinets, bassoon,
2 horns, 3 trumpets, timpani, and strings (organ *ad lib.*).

Duration: *c.*45 minutes

CONTENTS

PREFACE

Joseph Haydn's *Missa in Angustiis* (Hob. XXII:11), his so-called *Nelson Mass*, was composed in 1798 under difficult circumstances, as one of his few remaining duties of employment with the Esterhazy family. The first published edition, by Breitkopf & Härtel in 1803, was based on corrupt sources, yet it was this version that was used throughout the last century and well into the present one. During this period musical taste moved away from the early classicists and, coincidentally, 'orchestral' masses also fell into disfavour. In Protestant England, Haydn's great reputation—built on the success of his visits to London in the 1790s—quickly declined, and by 1850 he was remembered only as the composer of *The Creation* and a few symphonies.

The rehabilitation of the *Nelson Mass*, and of the composer's work in general, dates from the end of World War II. The first edition of the *Nelson Mass* to be based on Haydn's autograph was produced by H. C. Robbins Landon in 1963.[1] That same year also saw the appearance of the first recording of the work in its original orchestration, by the choir of King's College, Cambridge.[2] Two years later, in 1965, the Haydn Institut in Cologne published a further version.[3] Today, additional research and changing attitudes regarding performance practice have prompted the publication of this new edition to mark the 200th anniversary of the work's première.

Genesis

This work is the third of the so-called *Hermenegild* masses, written annually from 1796 to 1802 for the name-day of Maria Josefa, the wife of Prince Nicolaus Esterhazy. Although the autograph score is entitled simply 'Missa', Haydn entered the work in his *Entwurf-Katalog* as 'Missa in Angustijs'. This may be best translated as 'Mass in time of anxiety or constraint'. Such a title reflects the circumstances under which Haydn began work on 10 July 1798. Politically, it was an unsettled period in European history, dominated by Napoleon's campaigns against the Austro–Hungarian empire. The imperial government's inability to control inflation caused Haydn's patron, Prince Nicolaus, to introduce a number of household economies, including the dismissal of the courtly *Feldharmonie*, or wind-band octet, shortly before Haydn began to compose this mass. Faced with the loss of his woodwind players, the composer made the best of what was left—a small ensemble of strings, three trumpets, timpani, and solo organ to accompany the singers. Of these, the solo parts for two of the vocal quartet are exceptionally demanding. We know that the bass part was written for Conrad Specht, for whom Haydn had composed several operatic roles. Haydn must also have had a particular singer in mind for the soprano part, given its exceptional nature—possibly Barbara Pilhöfer, or alternatively Therese Gassmann, an established operatic soprano in Vienna, who was later to be associated by marriage with the Esterhazy household—but her true identity remains a mystery.

The first performance, on 23 September 1798 in Eisenstadt, did not go smoothly. At the last minute the venue was moved from the Bergkirche, where the Esterhazys normally worshipped, to the Stadtpfarr (parish) church, causing extra inconvenience for all concerned.

Title

As noted earlier, Haydn headed his score simply 'Missa', and also identified the work as 'Missa in Angustijs'. The main entry in his later catalogue is in Johann Elssler's script, to which the words 'Nelson Missa' have been added in an unknown hand. The now familiar title seems to have arisen from a visit Lord Nelson and Lady Hamilton made to Eisenstadt at the Esterhazys' invitation in September 1800. As the architect of the victory over Napoleon's fleet at Abukir two years earlier, Nelson was seen by the Austrians as a great hero. At Eisenstadt a number of works were performed in his honour, including this D minor mass. Haydn dined with the couple: they exchanged gifts, and by all accounts the meeting was a rich experience for all present.

Transmission during Haydn's lifetime

Following the successful publication of the score of *The Creation*, Breitkopf & Härtel pressed Haydn to provide them with more choral works with orchestra. Through his biographer Griesinger, the composer suggested a number of pieces including his early *Mass in F Major* (*Jugendmesse*, Hob. XXII:1) for which he added additional wind parts.[4] Also offered for consideration was the *Nelson Mass*, about which Griesinger wrote in these terms:

> Haydn told me that in the mass you wrote about he put the wind instruments into the organ part, because at that time Prince Esterhazy had dismissed the wind players. But he advises you to put everything that is obbligato in the organ part into the wind instruments and to print it that way.[5]

From this it could be argued that Haydn regarded his original orchestration, though very effective, as arising from reduced circumstances rather than from natural choice. There is a good arrangement with additional wind instruments in the Esterhazy archives which is thought to be by J. N. Fuchs. It was probably made after 1800, when the Prince had reinstated the wind players and when Haydn was less involved in the everyday administration of the Esterhazys' musical life. This orchestration is included in the *Joseph Haydn Werke* edition. Unfortunately, the Breitkopf edition of 1803—which did so much to popularize the mass—did not use this source. As a consequence it contains a number of distortions. The trumpet parts were rewritten, some of the text underlay was changed, and the string parts altered by the addition of non-authentic accents and slurs.

Modern edition

When Landon's version of the *Nelson Mass* appeared in 1963, it was a revelation. By going back to the autograph and other key sources, the editor uncovered major deficiencies in the Breitkopf score. Landon printed the original instrumentation (that is without wind instruments) and removed Breitkopf's editorial alterations, including the dubious rearrangement of the trumpet and timpani parts. Two years later, another modern edition appeared, this time edited by Günther Thomas for the Joseph Haydn Institut. The main difference between the German edition and Landon's was the inclusion in the former of the woodwind arrangement by Fuchs alongside Haydn's original instrumentation. It incorporates the clarinet and horn part omitted by Breitkopf, and offers a means by which the mass may also be performed in venues lacking a suitable organ.

This edition

This new edition of the *Nelson Mass* can be performed using either the original instrumentation (trumpets, timpani, strings, and organ), or with the additional wind instruments. In the latter case, the organ should act as a continuo instrument only.

Sometime after the première in 1798, Haydn appears to have modified the soprano and tenor lines to accommodate less able singers, scratching out several of the original notes in his autograph and replacing them with less demanding music. Both Landon and Thomas print these seemingly inferior versions, citing them as Haydn's authentic final revisions. Landon gives original passages as footnotes in his vocal score, while in Thomas's case, indication is only provided in the critical commentary. A typical example concerns the soprano part at bar 5 of the Gloria. Evidence from the authentic parts show that the soloist had originally the strong, simple melody which is echoed exactly by the chorus one bar later—this is surely the most effective. Haydn later altered his autograph copy to have four quavers on the first two beats and this is the reading printed in Günther Thomas's edition. The authority for Landon's different version of the same passage is not clear. The two adjustments to the solo tenor part at bars 18–20 and 23–24 which are printed in the main text of both publications are also clearly weaker.

This new edition aims to assist performers by offering guidance on these, and similar issues. As in several other settings, Haydn omits part of the text of the Credo: 'Et in unum Dominum Jesum Christum, Filium Dei, unigenitum' (Credo b. 31) and 'Qui ex Patre Filioque procedit' (Et Resurrexit b. 32).

The piano reduction in this vocal score is based on the orchestral parts. Editorial suggestions have been made regarding ornamentation. Capitalization and punctuation of the text have been modernized. Haydn's vocal slurs are also phrasing slurs; they are presented here as in the autograph material and, therefore, are not always consistent. The critical edition of the full score gives details on sources and variants. All indications in square brackets are editorial.

Scoring

Original version (1798):

3 trumpets, timpani, strings, and organ.

Revised version (Haydn/Fuchs *c.*1800):

Flute, 2 oboes, 2 clarinets, bassoon, 2 horns, 3 trumpets, timpani, and strings (organ *ad lib.*).

DENIS MCCALDIN
Lancaster/London 1995

NOTES
[1] Schott & Co., Edition 10808, (London: 1963).
[2] CD Recording Decca 421 146–2 [reissue from LP format].
[3] *Joseph Haydn Werke*, Reihe XXIII. Band 3, Messen Nr 9–10 (Munchen-Duisburg: 1965).
[4] See D. McCaldin, *Music Review*, 28 (1967), pp. 165–72, and Faber Music (London: 1993) for the author's performing edition.
[5] E. Olleson 'Georg August Griesinger's Correspondence with Breitkopf and Härtel', *Haydn Yearbook*, III (1965), p. 40.

VORWORT

Joseph Haydns *Missa in Angustiis* (Hob. XXII: 11), die soge-
nannte *Nelsonmesse*, wurde 1798 unter ungünstigen äußeren
Umständen als eine von wenigen verbliebenen Dienstpflichten
für die Esterhazy-Familie geschrieben. Die erste Druckausgabe,
die 1803 bei Breitkopf & Härtel herauskam, beruhte auf
verderbten Quellen. Dennoch wurde diese Ausgabe während
des ganzen letzten und weit bis in unser Jahrhundert hinein
benutzt. Der Wandel des musikalischen Geschmacks hatte im
Verlauf der Zeit zu einer Abwendung von den Klassikern
geführt, gleichermaßen waren 'Orchester'-Messen in Ungnade
gefallen. Im protestantischen England ließ Haydns enormes
Ansehen, das er sich durch die Erfolge bei seinen Londoner
Aufenthalte in den 1790er Jahren erworben hatte, rasch nach,
und um 1850 kannte man ihn allenfalls noch als den
Komponisten der *Schöpfung* und einiger weniger Sinfonien.

Erst nach dem 2. Weltkrieg gelangte die *Nelsonmesse*—wie
das Gesamtwerk des Komponisten—zu neuer Geltung. Eine
erste Ausgabe der *Nelsonmesse* auf Grundlage von Haydns
Originalpartitur legte H. C. Robbins Landon 1963 vor.[1] Im sel-
ben Jahr wurde das Werk durch den Chor des King's College
Cambridge erstmals in der originalen Besetzung auf Schallplatte
eingespielt.[2] Zwei Jahre später, 1965, gab das Joseph-Haydn-
Institut in Köln eine weitere Fassung heraus.[3] Neue
Forschungsergebnisse und ein geändertes Verständnis für his-
torische Aufführungspraxis machen heute, zur 200-Jahrfeier
der Uraufführung, eine Neuausgabe erforderlich.

Werkgeschichte

Die vorliegende Komposition ist die dritte der sogenannten
Hermenegild-Messen, die Haydn zwischen 1796 und 1802 Jahr
für Jahr zur Feier des Namenstags von Maria Josefa, Gemahlin
des Fürsten Nicolaus Esterhazy, schrieb. Zwar ist die autographe Partitur nur mit 'Missa' überschrieben, Haydn selbst
trug das Werk in seinen *Entwurf-Katalog* aber mit dem Titel
'Missa in Angustijs' ein. Dies kann vielleicht am besten mit
'Messe in einer Zeit von Furcht und Not' übersetzt werden. Der
Titel spiegelt die Umstände wider, unter denen Haydn die
Komposition des Werkes am 10. Juli 1798 in Angriff nahm. Die
politischen Verhältnisse waren damals in Europa hochgradig
ungeordnet; Napoleons Feldzüge gegen das Habsburgerreich
waren das bestimmende Ereignis. Dem Kaiserhaus gelang es
nicht, die Inflation in Grenzen zu halten, und so mußte Fürst
Nicolaus seinem Haushalt Beschränkungen auferlegen. Hierzu
gehörte die Entlassung der fürstlichen *Feldharmonie*, eines
Ensembles von acht Bläsern, kurz vor Beginn der Arbeit an der
neuen Messe. Da Holzblasinstrumente nicht länger zur Ver-
fügung standen, machte Haydn das Beste aus den verbliebenen
Kräften—einem kleinen Ensemble von Streichern, drei
Trompeten, Pauken, und obligater Orgel zur Begleitung der
Sänger. Zwei der Partien der Gesangssolisten sind besonders
anspruchsvoll. Man weiß, daß die Baßpartie für Conrad Specht
geschrieben wurde, den Haydn zuvor schon mehrmals mit
Opernrollen bedacht hatte. Haydn hatte sich, wie die
außergewöhnlichen Ansprüche an die Sängerin vermuten

lassen, auch eine bestimmte Stimme für die Sopranpartie
vorgestellt. In Frage kommen Barbara Pilhöfer oder auch
Therese Gassmann, eine angesehene Wiener Opernsängerin, die
später durch Heirat mit dem Hofstaat des Fürsten Esterhazy
verbunden war. Ihre wahre Identität bleibt aber weiterhin ein
Rätsel.

Die Uraufführung des Werkes am 23. September 1798 in
Eisenstadt verlief nicht ohne Probleme. In letzer Sekunde wurde
der Festgottesdienst von der Bergkirche, in der die Esterhazys
gewöhnlich die Messe zelebrierten, in die Stadtpfarrkirche ver-
legt, was neue Unannehmlichkeiten für die Aufführenden mit
sich brachte.

Werktitel

Wie oben bemerkt, versah Haydn die autographe Partitur mit
dem Titel 'Missa' und bestimmte sie an anderer Stelle näher als
'Missa in Angustijs'. Der Eintrag in seinem späteren
Werkverzeichnis, dem sogenannten *Haydn-Verzeichnis*,
stammt im wesentlichen von Johann Elssler; von fremder Hand
wurden dort die Worte 'Nelson Missa' hinzugefügt. Dieser
Titel, unter dem das Werk heute allgemein bekannt ist, scheint
auf den auf Einladung von Fürst Esterhazy erfolgten Besuch von
Lord Nelson und Lady Hamilton in Eisenstadt im September
1800 zurückzugehen. Die Österreicher sahen Lord Nelson
dank seiner Vedienste um den Sieg über Napoleons Flotte bei
Abukir im Jahre 1798 als einen Helden an. In Eisenstadt wurde
eine Reihe von Werken zu seinen Ehren gegeben, darunter die
d-Moll-Messe. Haydn speiste mit dem Paar zu Abend, sie über-
brachten sich gegenseitig Geschenke, und den Berichten zufolge
brachte die Begegnung allen Beteiligten unschätzbare
Erfahrungen.

Verbreitung zu Haydns Lebzeiten

Die Veröffentlichung der Partitur der *Schöpfung* war ein
außergewöhnlicher Erfolg. Breitkopf & Härtel drängten daher
den Komponisten, ihnen weitere Chorwerke mit Orchester zum
Druck zu überlassen. Durch Vermittlung von Georg August
Griesinger, seinem ersten Biographen, bot Haydn ihnen eine
Reihe von Stücken an, darunter seine Jugendmesse in F-Dur
(Hob. XXII: 1), die er mit zusätzlichen Bläserstimmen versah.[4]
Im Gespräch war aber auch die *Nelsonmesse*, über die
Griesinger folgendes mitzuteilen wußte:

> Haydn sagte mir, er habe in der Messe, wovon sie schrieben, die
> Blasinstrumente eigentlich auf die Orgel gesetzt, weil damals der
> Fürst Esterhazy die Spieler der blasenden Instrumente verab-
> schiedet hatte. Er rathe Ihnen aber, alles was in der Orgelstimme
> als obligat vorkommt, auf die Blasinstrumente übertragen und so
> druken zu lassen.[5]

Demnach könnte man annehmen, daß Haydn die Originalbesetzung, auch wenn sie als solche sehr wirkungsvoll ist,
nur als Notlösung aufgrund widriger Umstände und nicht als
seine freie künstlerische Entscheidung angesehen hat. Im
Esterhazy-Archiv ist eine wohlgelungene Bearbeitung mit zusätzlichen Bläserstimmen erhalten, als deren Urheber J. N. Fuchs

gilt. Sie stammt vermutlich aus der Zeit nach 1800, als der Fürst wieder Spieler von Blasinstrumenten besoldete und sich Haydn allmählich aus der Leitung des Musiklebens am Hofe der Esterhazys zurückzog. Diese Fassung wurde im Rahmen der *Joseph Haydn Werke* publiziert.

Leider beruht die Breitkopf-Ausgabe von 1803, die soviel dazu beigetragen hat, das Werk einer breiten Öffentlichkeit zugänglich zu machen, nicht auf dieser Vorlage. Hieraus geben sich eine Reihe von störenden Abweichungen zum Original. Die Trompetenstimmen wurden vereinfacht, die Textunterlegung ist teilweise geändert und die Streicherstimmen sind mit zahlreichen nicht-authentischen Vortragsbezeichnungen, Akzenten und Bindebögen, versehen.

Neuausgaben

Landon's Fassung der *Nelsonmesse* bedeutete bei ihrem Erscheinen eine Erleuchtung. Durch Heranziehung des Autographs und anderer Hauptquellen konnte der Herausgeber wesentliche Mängel der Breitkopf-Partitur aufdecken. Landon gab das Stück in Originalbesetzung—d.h. ohne die Bläserstimmen—wider und machte so die bei bei Breitkopf vorgenommenen editorischen Eingriffe, einschließlich der veränderten Trompeten- und Paukenstimmen, rückgängig. Zwei Jahre später erschien eine zweite Neuausgabe im Druck, diesmal herausgegeben von Günther Thomas am Joseph-Haydn-Institut. Der Hauptunterschied zur Ausgabe von Landon besteht in der Wiedergabe der von Fuchs eingerichteten Bläserstimmen als Zusatz zu Haydns originaler Besetzung. Hierin sind die Klarinetten- und Hornstimmen, die bei Breitkopf fehlen, eingeschlossen. Somit bietet sie die Möglichkeit, die Messe auch an Orten aufzuführen, an denen eine geeignete Orgel fehlt.

Zur vorliegenden Ausgabe

Die Neuausgabe der *Nelsonmesse* kann entweder mit der ursprünglichen Besetzung (Trompeten, Pauken, Streicher, und Orgel) oder mit den zusätzlichen Bläserstimmen aufgeführt werden. Entscheidet man sich für diese Fassung, so sollte die Orgel nur als Continuo-Instrument eingesetzt werden.

Zu einem nicht näher bestimmbaren Zeitpunkt nach der Uraufführung im Jahre 1798 hat Haydn offenbar die Sopran- und Tenorpartie verändert, um sie an weniger befähigte Sänger anzupassen. Hierzu radierte er einige Noten im Original aus und ersetzte sie durch weniger anspruchsvolle Passagen. Landon und Thomas halten sich an diese Lesarten, die zweifellos von geringerem musikalischen Wert sind, mit der Begründung, es handle sich um Haydns eigene endgültige Fassung. Landon gibt die ursprünglichen Lesarten als Fußnoten wider, während Thomas nur auf den Kritischen Bericht zur Ausgabe verweist. Ein charakteristisches Beispiel für diese Veränderungen ist der Sopranpart in Takt 5 des Gloria. Die

Originalstimmen belegen, daß der Solist ursprünglich die einfache eindrucksvolle Melodie sang, die der Chor im nächsten Takt als Echo aufgreift—sicherlich eine besonders wirkungsvolle Lösung. Haydn veränderte die erste Takthälfte im Autograph nachträglich in vier Achtelnoten; diese Fassung findet sich in der Ausgabe von Günter Thomas. Unklar bleibt, worauf die bei Landon wiedergegebene abweichende Fassung dieses Abschnitts beruht. Ähnlich bedeuten auch die im Solotenorpart vorgenommenen Änderungen in den Takten 18 bis 20 und 23—24, die in beiden Ausgaben als Haupttext erscheinen, eine erhebliche Schwächung des Originals. Die Neuausgabe will daher den Aufführenden bei diesen und ähnlichen Stellen klärende Hilfe anbieten. Wie in anderen Vertonungen des Ordinarium Missae hat Haydn Teile des Credo-Textes unberücksichtigt gelassen, und zwar die Abschnitte 'Et in unum Dominum Jesum Christum, Filium Dei, unigenitum' (Credo, nach T. 31) und 'Qui ex Patre Filioque procedit' (Et Resurrexit, nach T. 32).

Der Klavierauszug beruht auf den Orchesterstimmen. Vorschläge von seiten des Herausgebers beziehen sich vor allem auf die Verzierungen. Die Schreibweise des Textes, insbesondere Groß- und Kleinschreibung, und Zeichensetzung wurden modernisiert. Haydns Bögen in den Vokalstimmen bedeuten zugleich Phrasierungsbögen; sie folgen hier genau dem Befund des autographen Materials und sind deshalb nicht immer einheitlich gehandhabt. Der Kritische Bericht zur Partitur gibt im Detail Aufschluß über die Quellen und ihre Lesarten. Alle Angaben in eckigen Klammern stammen vom Herausgeber.

Besetzung

Ursprüngliche Fassung (1798):

3 Trompeten, Pauken, Streicher, und Orgel.

Revidierte Fassung (Haydn/Fuchs um 1800):

Flöte, 2 Oboen, 2 Klarinetten, Fagott, 2 Hörner, 3 Trompeten, Pauken und Streicher (Orgel *ad lib.*).

Übersetzt von Ulrich Leisinger

DENIS MCCALDIN
Lancaster/London 1995

ANMERKUNGEN

[1] Schott & Co., Nr. 10808, (London: 1963).

[2] Decca 421 146–2 (Neueinspielung auf CD).

[3] *Joseph Haydn Werke*, Reihe XXIII. Bd. 3, Messen Nr 9 und 10 (München-Duisburg: 1965).

[4] Siehe D. McCaldin, *Music Review* 28 (1967), S. 165—172, und die praktische Ausgabe durch den Autor bei Faber Music (London: 1993).

[5] *'Eben komme ich von Haydn' Georg August Griesingers Korrespondenz mit Joseph Haydns Verleger Breitkopf & Härtel 1799—1819*, hrsg. und komm. von Otto Biba, Zürich 1987, S. 175.

MISSA IN ANGUSTIIS
Nelson Mass

Edited by
Denis McCaldin

JOSEPH HAYDN (1732–1809)
Hob. XXII. 11

1. Kyrie

10

Nelson Mass

[1] In some sources, including the autograph, these voices enter here (see full score).

2. Gloria

16

¹ Later version (bb.18–19) gives ho - mi - ni-bus, which is how this figure should be interpreted generally. ² 'Later' version pax ho - mi - ni-bus

Nelson Mass

Nelson Mass

glo - ri - am tu - am, prop — ter glo - ri - am tu — am.

SOLO
Do - mi-ne De - us, Rex__ coe-le - stis, De — us Pa — ter,

De — us Pa — ter, Pa - ter om-ni — po-tens.

fz *fz* *p* *fz* *fz* *f*

3. Qui tollis

or ♪ to match violins, (and elsewhere)

¹ Sung

² Grace notes played before the beat

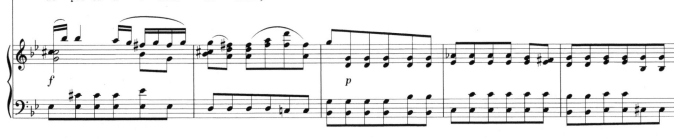

Nelson Mass

[1] Grace notes before the beat

4. Quoniam tu solus

[simile]

¹ Grace notes before the beat

5. Credo

¹ Text omitted—see Introduction to full score

Nelson Mass

Nelson Mass

6. Et incarnatus est

Nelson Mass

44

Nelson Mass

7. Et resurrexit

[1] Text omitted—see Introduction to full score

Nelson Mass

8. Sanctus

Nelson Mass

9. Benedictus

¹ Sung & played

² Sung & played

Nelson Mass

Nelson Mass

Nelson Mass

10. Agnus Dei

11. Dona nobis pacem

Nelson Mass

Nelson Mass

Nelson Mass

Music origination by
Barnes Music Engraving Ltd, East Sussex